Police File

Written by Jill Eggleton
Illustrated by Philip Webb

ST. VLADIMIR SCHOOL
7510-132 AVENUE
EDMONTON, AB T5C 2A9
TEL (780) 476-4613

I am Policeman Patty O'Donnell at the Piper Street Police Station. In my job, I get a lot of faxes, letters and e-mails. Read on to see what's on my files!

3 Baker Street
Timberlands
September 9

Policeman O'Donnell
Piper Street Police Station
Piper

Dear Policeman O'Donnell,

I have been having trouble with things going missing from around my house. Last week, someone took the birdbath and a tree from outside my window. This week, someone has taken the letter box. I have lost a lot of mail, and I have a big hole in the ground where the tree was! The birds have had to fly away to find another birdbath.

I know you are busy, but I would be very pleased if you could find the robber for me.

Yours sincerely,

D. Barnett

Black Beach
Hay Island
September 5

Dear Patty,

How are you getting on? I love being the police officer on this island. There are only ten people who live here and they are all well behaved. There is not much to do. Last week I saved a whale, and this week I rescued a bird that was caught in a fishing net. The rest of the time, I go fishing or sit in the sun.

I hope you have your new police car. I would like to hear from you, but I guess you are very busy. There is a lot more work to do in the city.

Maybe you could come and visit me soon.

Love from
Lacey

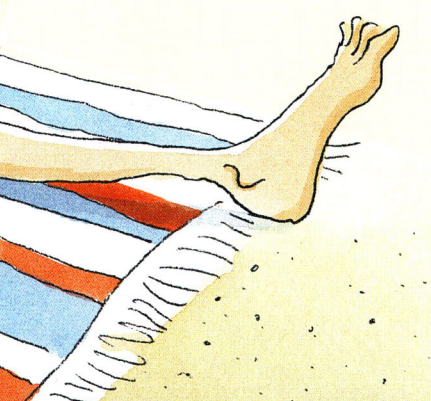

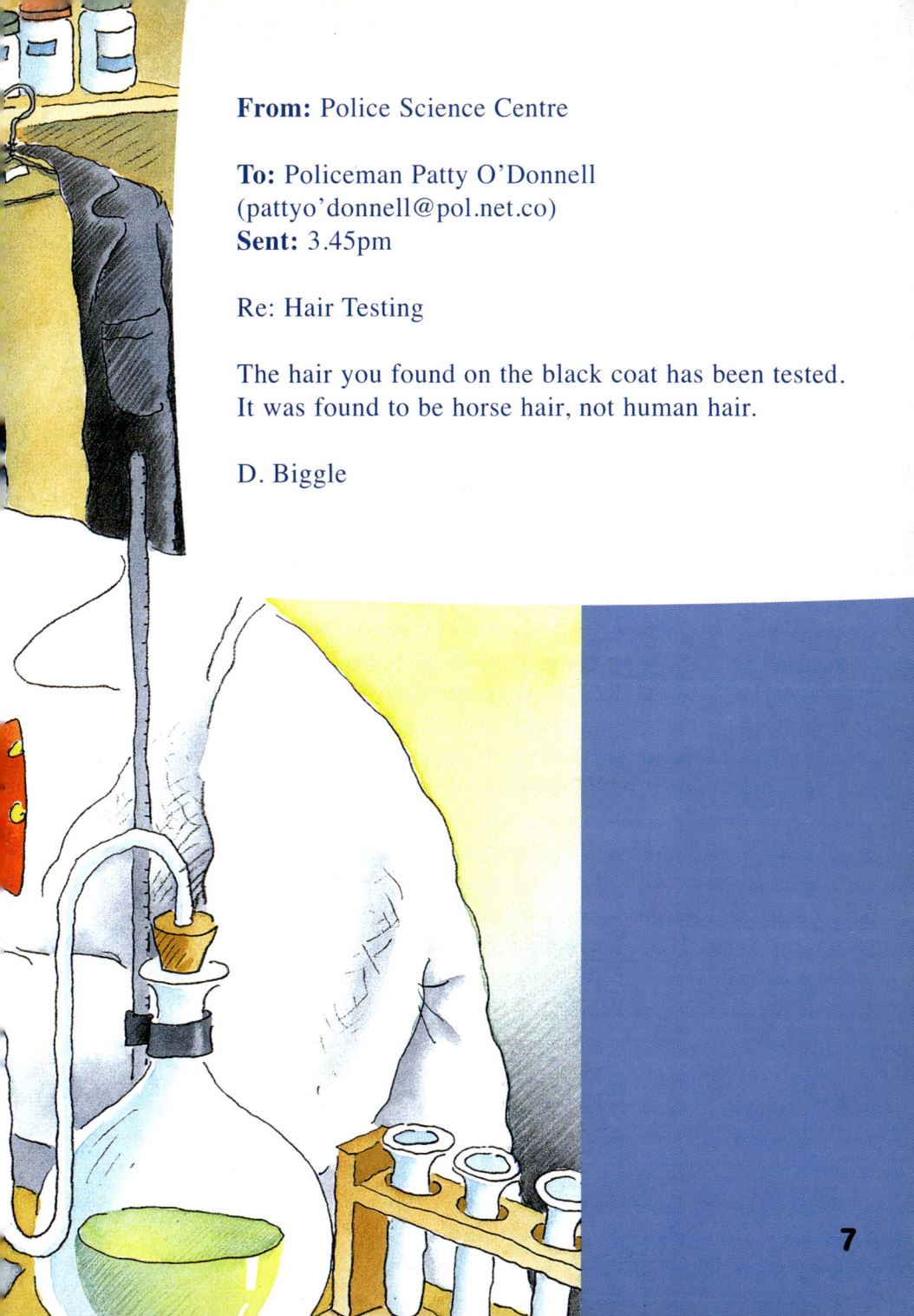

From: Police Science Centre

To: Policeman Patty O'Donnell
(pattyo'donnell@pol.net.co)
Sent: 3.45pm

Re: Hair Testing

The hair you found on the black coat has been tested. It was found to be horse hair, not human hair.

D. Biggle

Fax to: Constable Patty O'Donnell
From: Police Station Two
Date: 6.8. 2002

Re: Missing Pets

Please pin on noticeboard in the police station.

Parrot taken from cage at 21 Fork Street.

White dog - wearing a pink ribbon and a silver collar. Taken from 2 Bank Street.

Black cat last seen on the front step of 5 Green Street.

Three goldfish taken from 46 Dunk Lane.

Brown-and-white goat - last seen eating grass outside the Windsor's farm, Hill Road.

9

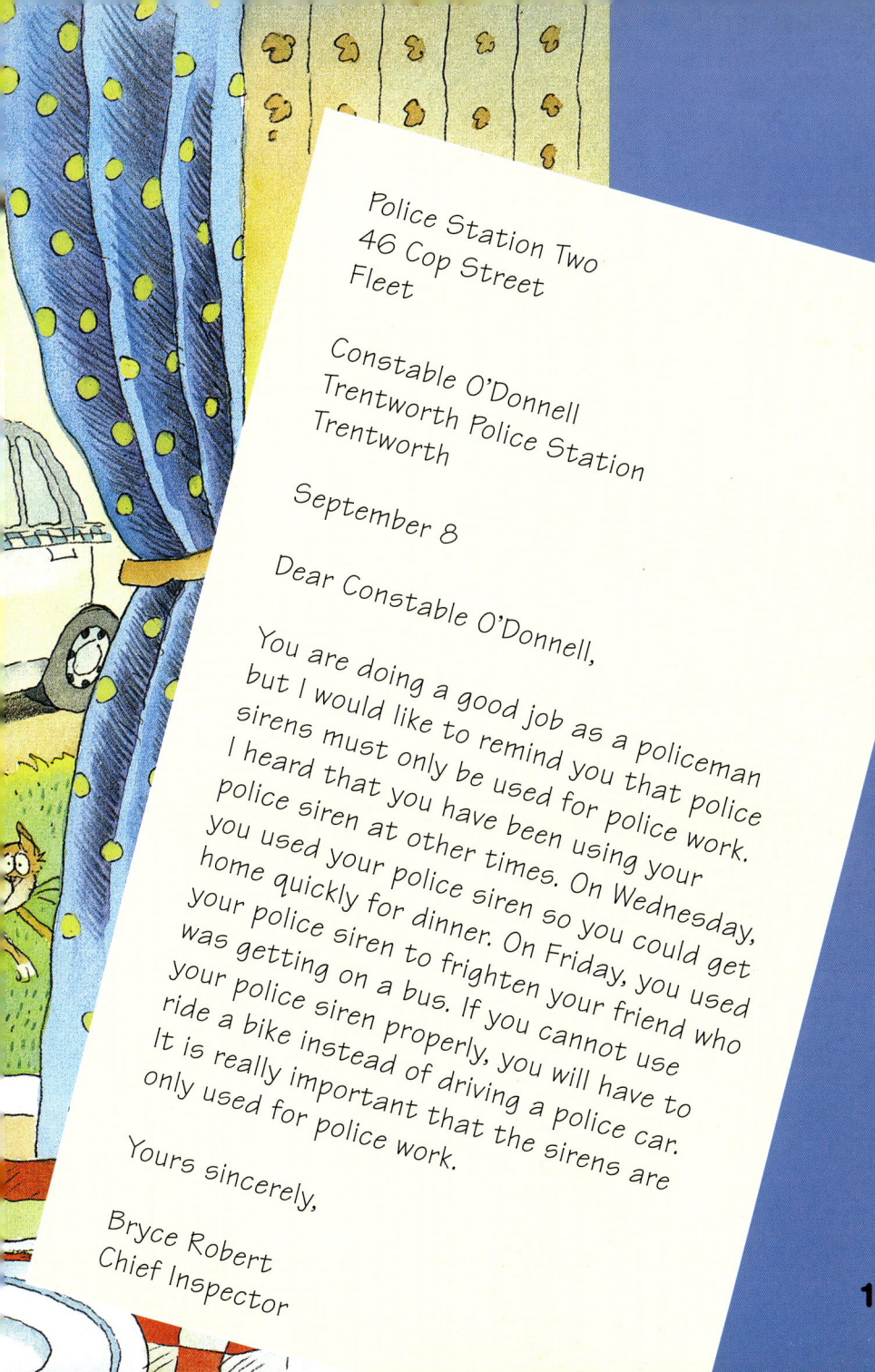

Police Station Two
46 Cop Street
Fleet

Constable O'Donnell
Trentworth Police Station
Trentworth

September 8

Dear Constable O'Donnell,

You are doing a good job as a policeman but I would like to remind you that police sirens must only be used for police work. I heard that you have been using your police siren at other times. On Wednesday, you used your police siren so you could get home quickly for dinner. On Friday, you used your police siren to frighten your friend who was getting on a bus. If you cannot use your police siren properly, you will have to ride a bike instead of driving a police car. It is really important that the sirens are only used for police work.

Yours sincerely,

Bryce Robert
Chief Inspector

27 Lung Avenue
Morrison

May 3

Dear Constable O'Donnell,

We would like to say sorry for writing on the wall of the police station. It was a very silly thing to do. We did not like having to spend all weekend scrubbing it off. Everybody who walked past growled at us, and we missed out on going to the beach party. Mum made us buy all the cleaning stuff with our own money. Now we can't go to the movies for four weeks. We will never write on walls again.

Yours sincerely,

Reeve and Callum

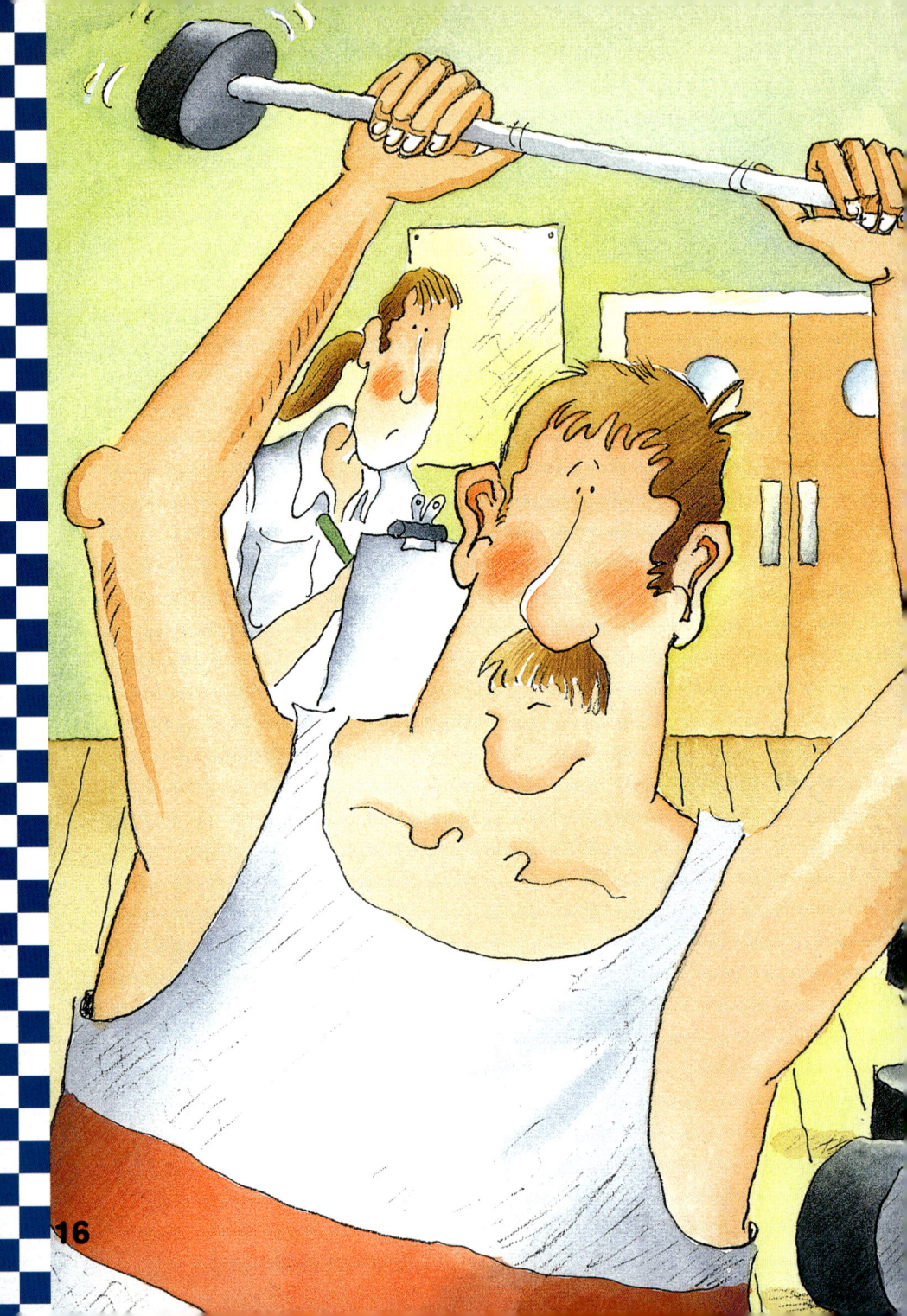

Police Fitness and Training Centre

Miller Mall
Malltown
23.5.

Dear Constable O'Donnell

Your next fitness test will be on Saturday July 6 at 10am. You will be tested in weightlifting, push-ups and speed running.

Please let us know if you cannot come for this test.

Yours sincerely,

Adelle Morris
Police Fitness Specialist

Mail

Letters, faxes and e-mails can:

Give information
Your next fitness test will be on Saturday July 6 at 10am.

Police Picnic, Robber Park, May 10

Ask questions
How are you getting on?

Apologise for something
We would like to say sorry for writing on the wall of the police station.

Request something
I know you are busy, but I would be very pleased if you could find the robber for me.

State facts
I have been having trouble with things going missing from around my house. Last week ...

Some letters start like this:
Dear Policeman O'Donnell

And end like this:
Yours sincerely

Some letters start like this:
Dear Patty

And end like this:
Love from

Some letters or faxes or e-mails are friendly
Dear Patty,
How are you getting on?

Some letters or faxes or e-mails are about business
Dear Constable O'Donnell,
You are doing a good job as a policeman but I would like to remind you that police sirens must only be used for police work.

Guide Notes

Title: Policeman's File
Stage: Launching Fluency

Text Form: Letters, Faxes, E-mails
Approach: Guided Reading
Processes: Thinking Critically, Exploring Language, Processing Information
Written and Visual Focus: Sending Messages

THINKING CRITICALLY
(sample questions)
- What letter do you think is from a friend? How can you tell?
- How else could Policeman Patty have been invited to the picnic?
- Which letter is a letter of apology?
- What information does the e-mail from the science centre give Patty?

EXPLORING LANGUAGE

Terminology
Spread, author and illustrator credits, ISBN number

Vocabulary
Clarify: investigate, sincerely, specialist, human
Nouns: police, file, station, siren
Verbs: fly, sit, test, wear
Singular/plural: policeman/policemen, pet/pets, movie/movies
Abbreviations: RSVP (please reply), am (before noon)

Print Conventions
Colon, apostrophes – possessive (Windsor's farm), contraction (can't)

Phonological Patterns
Focus on short and long vowel **o** (pr**o**blem, fr**o**m, b**o**x, g**o**, c**o**at)
Discuss base words – having, sitting, getting, fitness
Look at suffix **ly** (proper**ly**, quick**ly**)